The Case of the Incredible Expanding Molecules

Adapted by Thomas H. Hatch

Based on an original TV episode written and created by Tom Snyder, Bill Braudis, and David Dockterman

Illustrated by Bob Thibeault and Kristine Koob

Copyright © 1998 by Science Court, Inc.

Adapted by Thomas H. Hatch
from an original television show written and created by
Tom Snyder
Bill Braudis
David Dockterman
Produced by Tom Snyder Productions, Inc.

Published by Troll Communications L.L.C.

Science Court is a trademark of Science Court, Inc.
To Serve and Observe is a trademark of Science Court, Inc.

All rights reserved. No part of this book may be reproduced or utilized in any form or by any means, electronic or mechanical, including photocopying, recording, or by any information storage and retrieval system, without written permission from the publisher.

Created by Kent Publishing Services, Inc.
Designed by Signature Design Group, Inc.

Printed in the United States of America.

10 9 8 7 6 5 4 3 2 1

CRAMWOOD'S BIG CELEBRATION

Jen Betters had been looking forward to this assignment for weeks—not just because it meant she would be attending the party of the year, but also because she was hoping to interview some really big movie stars.

Jen's *Action News* van with the huge rooftop antenna and all the latest media-type equipment swung into the driveway of J. C. Cramwood's lavish white mansion. J. C. was the town's only movie star, and Jen—the town's only Science Court reporter—was sure she would find some of the star's famous pals at this special party.

Big spotlights cut wide paths across the ornate facade of Cramwood's fancy mansion, illuminating a banner that read "Welcome to the J. C. Cramwood Plaque-Unveiling Ceremony—Celebrating Cramwood's Movie Career." Jen saw that the notice continued in smaller but still quite prominent letters, "Please wipe your feet!"

"Same old J. C. Cramwood," Jen told her driver. "He's unveiling a plaque of himself that he'll dedicate to himself in honor of himself. Mister Big Deal. He must like himself, I guess, just because he's the only movie star ever to come out of this town. His head is so big he can't find a hat that will fit it."

As the van inched its way through the throng, Jen kept her reporter's eye out for celebrities to interview, but the only people she recognized were a few of her Science Court friends. There were attorneys Doug Savage and Alison Krempel; Stenographer

Fred; Alison's assistant, Tim; and Micaela, the smart girl who attends every Science Court trial.

Jen and her crew worked their way through the crowd and mounted the front steps of Cramwood's magnificent house. With cameras rolling, Jen turned toward the lens and, with the towering columns of the Cramwood mansion as her backdrop, announced to her TV audience that the unveiling would take place in just a few minutes. The group entered the foyer and found their way to the auditorium, where J. C. himself was on a stage in front of a canvas draped over a large stand. A sign on the wall asked, "Did you wipe your feet?"

Nobody ever accused J. C. Cramwood of being polite, or modest, thought Jen just as Cramwood seized the moment and proudly announced that the unveiling was about to begin.

"Without further ado, I present to you . . . ME!" shouted Cramwood as he pulled the cord and dropped the canvas. Ooohs, ahhhs, and enthusiastic applause erupted from the audience as the plaque, framed beautifully in dark wood and bearing Cramwood's likeness, was revealed.

CLUNK. WHIRR. HUM. BUZZ. The transformers switched on as spotlights filled the stage with a golden glow. "Stand up and please take a bow, Sonya Sondheim," said Cramwood, encouraging the excited crowd to recognize the sculptor for her work.

"Bravo," shouted the crowd.

"That's enough, Sonya, sit down. Now turn on more lights!" J. C. directed. More clunks, whirrs, hums, and buzzes filled the room as the golden glow turned brilliant white with hundreds of hot spotlights aimed at Cramwood's likeness.

2

THE HOT SPOT

The heat from the spotlights was intense. J. C. Cramwood started to sweat as he stood beneath the plaque. In fact, the auditorium was getting so hot that the cheese and crackers placed on the tables in the back were being transformed into a gooey mess. People were starting to walk out. Cramwood announced that everyone should stay and that there was surely enough cheese and crackers for everyone to have one, but no more. And he'd be delighted to answer any questions that might be on anyone's mind.

It was Tim, assistant Science Court

attorney, who noticed the problem first. The brass plaque bearing J. C.'s likeness, which had seemed perfectly matched to its frame, now appeared to rest uncomfortably in it. The frame looked too small, and Tim saw that it was beginning to crack.

Tim raised his hand and called out, "Excuse me, but I think the plaque is falling." Everyone in the room gasped. The brass plaque was, indeed, bulging and seemed to be straining against the frame. Cramwood noticed it, too, and reached up to hold it when all of a sudden, the plaque popped out of its frame, tumbled toward the stage, and landed squarely on top of J. C. Cramwood.

Doug Savage, Science Court attorney, was in the back of the auditorium when all the commotion occurred onstage. He was more interested in the cheese and crackers than in J. C.'s question-and-answer session. But, like the rest of the audience, he heard the crack of

the splitting frame and saw the plaque crash and pin Cramwood to the floor. Unlike the rest of the audience, who began to clear out of the overheated space, Doug went up to the front of the room to see if he could help.

Doug and J. C. were alike in many ways. Both had lots of hair, big white teeth, and high opinions of themselves. Doug thought he smelled an opportunity as he helped Cramwood crawl out from under the heavy plaque. The room emptied out, and he and J. C. were left alone sitting on the edge of the stage.

"Hey, Cramwood, thanks for a great night," said Doug. "That was really cool the way that plaque came crashing down."

"Uh, you're welcome. Glad to oblige. Anything for a fan," replied J. C.

"Boy, it's really hot up here," commented Doug.

"Yeah, it's the spotlights. I wanted to

make sure everyone could see the plaque. I look totally great in brass."

"Well, I think everybody saw it, all right, especially when it fell on top of you. What a dangerous stunt. Do you do all of your own stunts in your movies?" asked Doug.

J. C. gave Doug a long look. "It wasn't a stunt, pal. That plaque wasn't supposed to fall."

"But it could have killed you. I thought it was just another part of the show."

"I have been in some dangerous, death-defying scenes in some of my movies, but this is real life, and I'm scared. I want my mommy," sobbed J. C.

"It's okay, don't cry," said Doug. "Boy, I'm really surprised that frame failed to hold the plaque. Sonya Sondheim is supposed to be a very good artist, and she should have known better than to put a heavy brass plaque in such a skimpy frame."

"You really think so?" asked J. C. as he choked back his sobs.

"Yeah, I do think so. And what's more, I think you're a victim of Sonya's faulty framing. Yeah, that's it. You've been made into a fool by a flimsy, faulty frame job, and we're going to sue Sonya for serious bucks in Science Court!" Doug declared. "What do you say, J. C.?"

"Works for me, Doug."

THE ARTIST'S ANXIETY

Sonya Sondheim's sculpture studio looked more like a machine shop than a place where beautiful art was created. There were power tools of all sorts spread around the room, pulleys and blocks suspended from the ceiling for lifting heavy metal objects, scrap iron and wood piled in the corners. Sonya was wearing a welder's mask and standing over her workbench heating something with a blowtorch. She couldn't even hear Alison Krempel and her assistant, Tim, as they opened the door and walked into the studio.

"Wow!" exclaimed Tim.

"Hello . . . ? Hello, Sonya Sondheim, hello," shouted Alison. Sonya turned off her blowtorch and welcomed the two Science Court attorneys, talking through her mask.

Alison did not understand what Sonya was saying until Sonya raised her mask and apologized. "Oh, I'm so sorry. You must be Alison Krempel and Tim. I'm very glad you could come."

"What are you making, Ms. Sondheim?" asked Tim. "I love sculpture."

"Actually, Tim, they're cookies! Not exactly art, but they sure do taste good."

WOULD YOU LIKE TO TRY THEM? BE CAREFUL, THEY'RE HOT.

"They're awesome! Blowtorch cookies, mmm," said Tim as he gobbled some up.

Alison was hesitant about meeting with the sculptor who had created the framed plaque that had fallen on J. C. Cramwood. Alison had received a phone call from Sonya that morning. Something about being sued by Cramwood for faulty framing, Sonya had said. But Alison wasn't so sure she wanted to be involved with this case. After all, she had seen the plaque fall right out of its frame herself. She was an eyewitness and wasn't sure she could tell who had been at fault.

"So what's this suit about? How much is Cramwood suing you for?" asked Alison.

It seemed that Cramwood didn't want money at all. He wanted Sonya to create a two-hundred-foot-tall statue of him. Sonya told Alison and Tim that having to create such a statue would ruin her. Not only would she have to pay for all that brass, but creating such an object would take months of her time, and she wouldn't be able to work on any of her other art. "Besides," Sonya emphasized, "the plaque was a perfect fit for that frame. I checked it myself, and I know it was perfect when I installed it up on the stage."

"Well, Sonya, I was at the ceremony, too, and I thought the plaque looked too big for the frame," Alison admitted.

"Me too, Sonya," said Tim. "The plaque was bulging right out of that little wooden frame. Tell me, if you lose this lawsuit, will you still have time to make blowtorch cookies?"

"Absolutely not. My life will stop while I create that ridiculous giant brass statue. J. C. Cramwood's attorney, Doug Savage, dropped off the specifications for the statue yesterday. Listen to this, 'If found guilty, you, Sonya Sondheim, will make a life-size statue of J. C. Cramwood that is two hundred feet high.' How's that for nerve? I just can't figure out what happened. I measured right down to the millimeter when I built that frame. Maybe somebody broke it on purpose. You've just got to help me, Alison. Please."

"You mean, J. C. Cramwood believes a two-hundred-foot-tall statue is life-size? I knew he thought he was bigger than life, but this is ridiculous," said Alison. "And did you just say that Doug Savage is Cramwood's attorney? Now there's a pair," she added.

"Can Science Court make Sonya do this if she is found to have been responsible for the accident, Alison?" asked Tim. "I'd sure hate to wait years for more of these cookies."

"I'm afraid so, Tim," Alison replied. "Okay, Sonya, we'll help you. I'm not sure how yet, but we'll find a way."

COURTROOM CONUNDRUM

Jen Betters charged up the courtroom steps with her camera crew trailing behind. It was the opening day of the *Cramwood vs. Sondheim* trial, and Jen was reporting live from the scene. As she approached the top of the steps, she noticed Fred, the court stenographer, wearing a smock and beret, standing in front of an easel, and holding a palette filled with blobs of brilliant blue, red, and indigo paint.

Fred was squinting one eye tightly and, with outstretched arm and extended thumb, appeared to be trying to bring his distant subject matter into his line of sight. Fred looked more like a portrait painter than a court stenographer. Jen stopped to admire Fred's painting, which she found curious at best. "Wow, looks interesting, Fred. But kind of blurry."

"Yeah, I know," answered Fred. "Guess I'm a better typist than painter, but I'm working on it. I've always wanted to be a courtroom artist. If I get good enough at sketching courtroom scenes, I'll sell them to you for your broadcast reports from Science Court. What do you think, Jen? Interested?"

Jen was already on her way through the columned entrance to the courthouse, but she called back, "Sure, Fred. Keep up the good work and we'll see if we can use your stuff. Have your people call my people."

Thirty minutes later, Jen and her camera crew were positioned outside the courtroom door. Fred, sketchbook in hand, had taken his place inside the courtroom and was calling the court into session. As he announced the Honorable Judge Stone, he looked at her past his outstretched arm and extended thumb.

"Fred, what are you doing?" asked Judge Stone.

"Thought I might try sketching the trial, Judge. Your face would look great on Jen Betters's six o'clock news report."

"Okay, Fred, as long as you can still record what everybody says. So, today we have movie star J. C. Cramwood suing Sonya Sondheim, claiming that when her faulty framing failed, he wound up plastered under the plaque. Is that about right, guys?"

"Yup, Your Honoress," said Fred.

"Then proceed, Mr. Savage, with your opening remarks, please."

"Thank you, Judge Stone. Ladies and gentlemen of the jury, my client, J. C. Cramwood, is a famous movie star. He's probably the most famous person to come out of this town. But because of Sonya Sondheim's shoddy work, a brass plaque fell on top of him at an important ceremony, causing him untold embarrassment. We will prove that Sonya is at fault and will ask that you order her to make an elaborate two-hundred-foot-tall statue of Mr. Cramwood to pay him back for all his troubles."

"Ms. Krempel, your remarks, please," announced the judge.

"Thank you, Your Honor. We will show that the incident at the Cramwood ceremony was not a reflection of Sonya Sondheim's workmanship, but rather the result of a scientific principle."

Doug Savage, who was convinced he had an easy, open-and-shut case, called his first and only witness—J. C. Cramwood.

"Tell the court, Mr. Cramwood, did a brass plaque made by Sonya Sondheim fall on you?" asked Doug.

"Yes."

"Was it supposed to?" Doug inquired.

"No," said J. C.

"Your witness, Ms. Krempel."

"No questions," Alison responded.

"I rest my case, Your Honor," Doug announced confidently.

"Not much of a case, is it, Doug? Ms. Krempel, the floor's all yours," said the judge.

Alison Krempel quickly took a different approach to the case. She decided to present actual evidence and expert witnesses. The first person called to the stand was Dr. Julie Bean, materials expert.

Julie testified that she had examined the scene right after the accident and had found a plaque made of brass, a broken frame made of wood, and spotlights that were extremely hot. She went on to say that there could be a simple scientific explanation as to why the plaque looked like it was too big for the frame.

"The heat from the lights caused the particles that make up the plaque . . . " she began.

"Objection," Doug yelled. "I examined that plaque myself, and it's not made of particles or pieces of any kind. It's completely solid."

"You're just not looking closely enough!" Alison retorted.

"Okay, take it easy. Maybe it's a good time for a recess," said the judge.

Meanwhile, outside the courtroom door, Jen was speaking into the microphone. "I have to admit, that plaque sure looked solid to me. Could it actually be made up of particles? We'll find out when we return to all the action at Science Court."

Fred was at her side as soon as the camera lights were switched off. "So, do you like my sketch, Jen? Can you use it for the six o'clock news?"

JULIE BEAN'S IDEA

Fred was crushed by Jen's reply—but not in the same way that J. C. Cramwood had been when the plaque fell on him. Fred was heartbroken because Jen made it clear she didn't like his sketches. So as Judge Stone called Science Court to order, Fred went back to being the great stenographer he was. Dr. Julie Bean continued her testimony.

Julie explained that everything in the universe is made up of very tiny particles called atoms and molecules.

"Adam . . . ? Who's Adam?" interrupted a confused Doug Savage. Doug was often confused, and Judge Stone knew it. To keep him from being embarrassed by a rival attorney, she suggested that Micaela, who was a frequent member of the Science Court audience, help Doug understand atoms. Micaela explained that atoms are the smallest parts of any element, and that they work like building blocks. Atoms that are alike fit together to form elements; atoms of different types can combine to form molecules.

Doug said he got it, and Dr. Julie Bean went on. She pointed out that heat has a very interesting effect on these tiny particles of matter. In fact, she had devised a demonstration to show the court the effect of heat on matter. Julie pulled out a small piece of brass, the same material as the plaque, and a measuring device that could detect even slight changes in size. Then she asked for the heat in the room to be turned up.

Realizing that it was going to take quite a while for the large, drafty courtroom to get

hot enough, Julie asked Judge Stone if she could perform the demonstration in a smaller room. When the judge couldn't think of another room to use, Fred quickly suggested the judge's chambers.

"That would be perfect," said Julie.

The judge protested that her office was too small and too messy. But the cause of justice prevailed, and all the members of the court tromped into Judge Stone's chambers, much to her discomfort. Everyone was excited about the chance to see the judge's private office, especially the jurors, who began cheering and chanting. Because they had been stuck in a jury box all morning, they welcomed almost any change.

Everyone went, including Jen Betters, who brought her camera, microphone, and entire crew. Everyone, that is, except Sonya Sondheim, who quietly stayed back in the courtroom. She was too nervous thinking about having to create that two-hundred-foot statue of J. C. Cramwood. Making blowtorch cookies had always helped Sonya forget her troubles, so she pulled out her ingredients and equipment and whipped up a batch right then and there.

THE JUDGE'S CHAMBERS

Judge Stone's chambers were cluttered with pieces of her life history. There were old textbooks from her college and law-school days, cabinets lined with trophies and awards, and lots of toys. Yes, toys. Judge Stone loved racing cars, and little figures of army men all lined up ready for battle, and dolls with dresses and hair you can groom. She also loved sports, and there were baseball mitts and hockey sticks and football jerseys and pennants from her favorite teams among the books and toys.

Now the room was filled with people, and the temperature was already rising because all those bodies were packed in so close to one another. Doug Savage and J. C. Cramwood started to sweat when they saw Julie Bean's demonstration set up on the judge's desk. It looked real official and real scientific. They wondered what it could possibly prove. The piece of brass had been placed on top of the measuring device, and the pointer was poised to move if even the slightest change in size occurred.

Judge Stone asked Fred to turn up the heat in the room to its highest setting, and they all held their breath waiting to see what would happen. As the room got hotter, Doug, J. C., Fred, the judge, and the others started to sweat even more. Fred began to look over Judge Stone's trophies displayed in the cabinets.

"What did you win this track medal for, Judge Stone?" asked Fred.

"Track," said the judge.

Track, Fred said to himself. *That makes me think. If a track athlete can become a judge, then why can't a stenographer become an artist?* And so, with renewed determination, Fred whipped out his sketchbook and got to work.

The sketching went well, even though the judge's chambers were very crowded. Maybe it went well because everyone was so still. In fact, it was so hot that everyone was almost asleep. Everyone, that is, except Julie Bean.

"Look, look. The pointer is starting to move," she said. The people in the room suddenly woke up.

"Oooh, ahhh," they all exclaimed as they saw the pointer slowly shift. "What do you suppose this means?"

"Water . . . water!" Doug pleaded. "Your Honor, I can't stand it any longer. It's just too hot in here," he gasped, hoping to shift the attention away from the moving pointer.

"Waters all around, Fred," ordered the judge. "Doug, you'll live. Dr. Bean, please enlighten us as to the meaning of your demo, and make it snappy. The jury is about to doze off again."

Julie explained, "The heat is causing the tiny particles in the brass to move around each other faster and faster. As the particles move faster, they take up more space. So the brass starts to get bigger. It expands."

"Just the same way the brass plaque expanded when J. C. Cramwood ordered all those very hot spotlights turned on?" asked Alison Krempel.

"Yes," said Julie.

"Could the brass plaque have expanded enough to pop out of its wooden frame?" Alison continued.

"Again, yes. Absolutely," answered Julie Bean.

HOT
COLD
WHEN HEAT IS APPLIED TO AN OBJECT, THE ATOMS IN THE OBJECT BEGIN TO MOVE FASTER. AS THE ATOMS MOVE FASTER, THEY TAKE UP MORE SPACE, SO THE OBJECT EXPANDS.

"And what happened when the brass cooled down?" Alison asked.

Julie thought before she replied. "Well, the particles slowed down, and the thing got smaller again."

"Objection, Your Honor," Doug broke in. "I'm too hot to think about all this complicated tiny, big, hot, cool, fast, slow stuff."

"You got it, Doug. Let's get back into the courtroom, and somebody turn on the air conditioning," ordered Judge Stone.

As the group tromped back into the courtroom, Fred stopped to show Jen his sketch. "Better, Ms. Betters?" he asked with a hopeful smile.

"Keep trying, Fred," she advised.

DR. FULLERGHAST EXPLAINS

Back in the courtroom, Judge Stone banged her gavel and asked how the jury felt. Everyone was much more comfortable now, and the jury was refreshed and reenergized after Sonya passed around her blowtorch cookies. Fred ate several. *Hmm*, he thought, *if a sculptor can be a cookie baker, then why can't a stenographer be . . .* Doug Savage interrupted Fred's thought by announcing that he had new evidence that would blow the case wide open.

Judge Stone reminded him that he had already rested his case. But Doug was not to be stopped. "Rested, Your Honor?" he responded.

"Yes, my case rested nicely while we were in your warm, cozy chambers. But now my case is wide awake and ready to move forward."

"Go ahead, Doug," Judge Stone said with a shrug of her shoulders. So Doug called the famous materials expert Dr. Henry Fullerghast to the stand.

"Now, Dr. Fullofgas . . ." Doug began.

"That's Fullerghast," the good doctor corrected him.

"Now, Henry, could you please tell the jury if it's true that brass expands when it is heated, and if, in your opinion, it is possible for a brass plaque to expand enough to pop out of its frame."

Dr. Fullerghast responded that it was indeed possible for such a thing to happen. And when Doug asked him to describe other things that expand when they are heated, the doctor proceeded to conduct a scientific demonstration of his own.

The jury watched with fascination as he produced a Bunsen burner, a plastic bag, and a thermometer. Dr. Fullerghast held the air-filled plastic bag just high enough above the flame to avoid setting it on fire—but still close enough to heat the air inside it. The bag seemed to expand and rise up above the flame. Similarly, when he held the thermometer above the flame, the mercury inside began to rise in its tube.

Dr. Fullerghast explained that both the air and the mercury were expanding as they got hotter. "In fact, this is exactly what happened to J. C. Cramwood's brass plaque, as well as the frame it was in. Both expanded as they heated up," continued the doctor.

This latest testimony was beginning to undermine Alison Krempel's case, and she was nervous. She could tell what was coming next. Everything she had tried to establish with Julie Bean's testimony was now being turned around and used against her. She was angry at Doug for being smarter than she thought he was. But she wasn't quite sure what to do. Tim was worried, too, but he had an idea. It was a long shot, but he went over to confer quietly with Professor Parsons, another scientific expert, while Doug continued questioning his witness.

"So, Dr. Fullerghast, let me understand what was happening here. The brass plaque was expanding, but so was its frame. They were both getting bigger at the same time?" Doug was beside himself with excitement at his own brilliant deduction.

"Well, yeah," said the doc.

"Then the plaque shouldn't have fallen out of its frame unless it was just too big for it to begin with, right?" shouted Doug. "Boy! Am I good!" he added.

"Well, I can't comment on the quality of Ms. Sondheim's work. I'm a scientist, not a sculptor," responded Dr. Fullerghast. "But I can say without reservation that both the brass plaque and the wooden frame it was in expanded as the room heated up."

Doug was elated, and he assured his witness that he had been of great help before he turned him over to Alison Krempel.

Alison looked at Tim and shrugged as if to say, "What are we going to do now?" Every member of the jury was obviously impressed with Dr. Fullerghast's testimony,

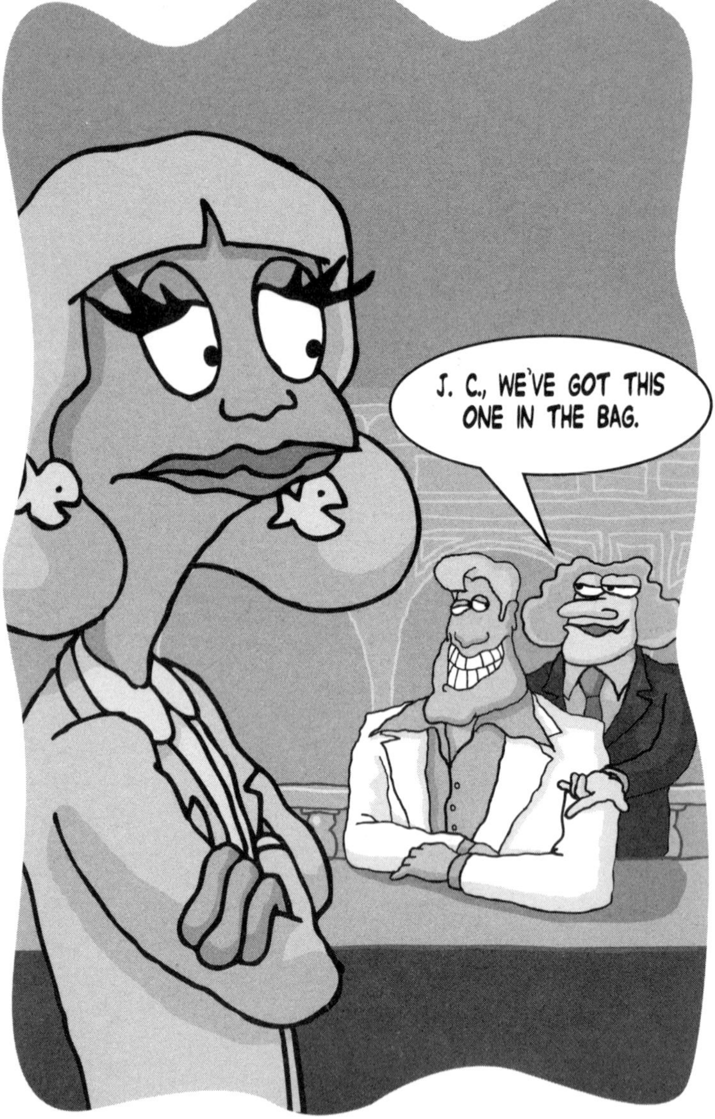
J. C., WE'VE GOT THIS ONE IN THE BAG.

and they cheered for him. Doug grinned from ear to ear and slapped J. C. Cramwood on the back. Alison didn't know what to say when Judge Stone asked her if she had any questions for Fullerghast. She hesitated for a moment. Cramwood was about to start passing out cigars to celebrate his victory.

Then, suddenly, Tim took charge. He addressed the court and said that, while they had no questions for Dr. Fullerghast, they would call Science Court's favorite witness, Professor Parsons, to the stand.

PROFESSOR PARSON'S TESTIMONY

Professor Parsons rose out of the packed courtroom audience and stepped forward to take his oath. He swore to do his best to uphold the principles of Science Court—where science is the law and scientific thinking rules. Alison stood alongside Tim and Sonya, hoping she could come up with a new plan. Her case had been damaged by Fullerghast's testimony, and she could see that the jury had serious doubts about whether it was really heat expansion or simply shoddy workmanship that had caused the plaque to plunge from its frame and land on J. C. Cramwood.

Tim leaned over to Alison and whispered, "Ask him about the thermostat." Alison wasn't quite sure what Tim meant, but she had come to appreciate his ideas and insights. She knew he wouldn't let her down, and she seemed to regain some of her customary confidence as she approached the professor.

She started by reminding the court that everyone had just heard the testimony of Dr. Julie Bean and Dr. Fullerghast that things expand when they're heated. "What do you think of the testimony you've heard so far, Professor?" Alison asked.

"They're both correct. Good people, those two," responded the professor.

"Well, then," Alison continued, "why would the plaque pop out of the frame if the brass and the wood were both expanding?"

Silence. No one in the courtroom said a word for several moments. Everyone was thinking about Alison's question, trying to

WHY WOULD THE PLAQUE POP OUT OF THE FRAME IF THE BRASS AND THE WOOD WERE BOTH EXPANDING?

answer it in his or her own way. Even the professor paused before answering.

Could it be that there was some other material in the framing that didn't expand? No, Dr. Fullerghast had testified that all materials expand when heat is applied. Could it be that the brass heated up and the wood didn't? No, the lights were shining on both materials at the same time. Could it be that invisible creatures from Mars pushed the brass plaque out of its frame and onto J. C. Cramwood because they thought he was a conceited jerk? Well, maybe.

It was Doug Savage who broke the silence. "Whoa, time-out. I don't want to hear the answer to that question."

"Mr. Savage, there's no such thing as a time-out in Science Court. Objections, yes. Recess, yes. But time-outs, no. Now, why don't you want the witness to answer?" asked Judge Stone.

"Because it might hurt my case, and I want to win," Doug said.

"Mr. Savage, you're just delaying the inevitable. Professor, answer the question, please."

"Easy," said Professor Parsons confidently. "Different things expand different amounts."

"I'm doomed," Doug cried, banging his head on the table. The jurors murmured enthusiastically and shifted in their seats. They were ready to listen attentively to the professor's explanation.

"You see," Professor Parsons went on, "tiny basic particles, such as atoms and molecules, are arranged slightly differently in different things. Therefore, everything expands a different amount when heated."

"Ask him about the thermostat," Tim whispered to Alison again. But before she could, Professor Parsons had whipped out a strip of metal that was a shiny silver color on

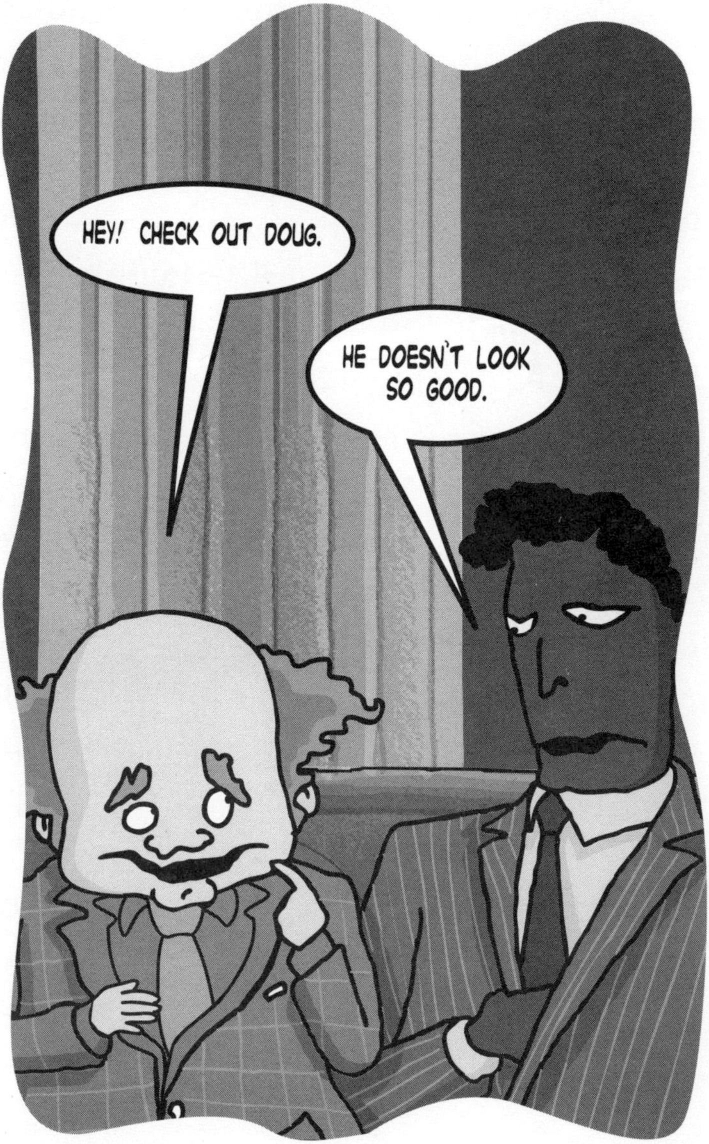
HEY! CHECK OUT DOUG.
HE DOESN'T LOOK SO GOOD.

one side and a dull yellow color on the other.

"Please allow me to demonstrate. Dr. Fullerghast, may I borrow your Bunsen burner?" asked Parsons. Fullerghast handed him the burner, and Professor Parsons started heating up the strip of metal. "Don't try this at home, folks. I'm a trained professional. Anybody got any marshmallows or wieners?"

While the professor was laughing at his own joke, the strip of metal started bending to one side. "The thermostat, Alison, don't forget to ask him about the thermostat!" Tim whispered. Doug, who was frantically searching through his briefcase looking for marshmallows, didn't notice the excitement building in the courtroom. Ooohs and ahhhs came not only from the jury box but from the audience as well.

"What's going on?" cried someone in the gallery.

"Well," said Professor Parsons, "one side of this strip is steel and the other is brass. The

THIS STRIP HAS TWO DIFFERENT KINDS OF METAL. THAT'S IMPORTANT TO KNOW WHEN I HEAT IT UP.

two metals are expanding at different rates, causing the strip to bend."

"This is how a thermostat works, right?" interrupted Tim, who couldn't wait anymore.

"Mine works by turning the dial," said Doug.

Professor Parsons explained, "That's how you set a thermostat. But most thermostats in people's homes have strips made from different metals inside them. As the air in the house gets hotter or colder, the strips bend back and forth, pushing the on/off button on your furnace. Pretty neat, huh?"

"Yeah, that's pretty neat, but I win the case if brass and wood expand at the same rate," said Doug, who was still hopeful.

"Well, brass and wood don't," replied Professor Parsons.

"It's okay, I can still win," insisted Doug.

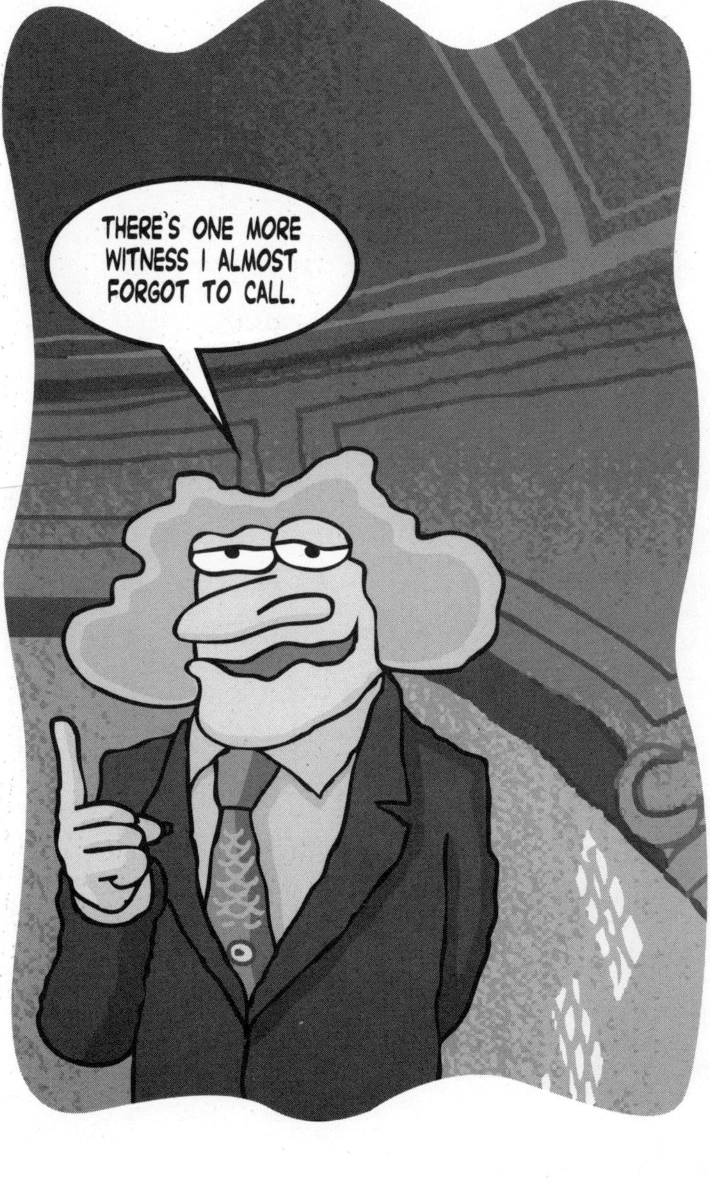
THERE'S ONE MORE WITNESS I ALMOST FORGOT TO CALL.

SONYA TAKES THE STAND

"Jen Betters here, reporting live from just outside the magnificent oak-paneled entrance to Judge Gwendolyn Stone's courtroom, where the *Cramwood vs. Sondheim* trial is in full swing. Doug Savage, attorney for movie star J. C. Cramwood, appears to be searching for a new explanation as to why the brass plaque made by sculptor Sonya Sondheim fell out of its frame.

"Doug's original claim that Sonya Sondheim built a frame that was too small to hold the plaque seems to have been successfully challenged by a string of dramatic scientific evidence. This evidence suggests that Cramwood's use of very hot spotlights caused the brass plaque and the wood frame to expand at different rates, making the plaque literally burst out of its frame and land on Cramwood. But does the jury believe it?

"There's a lot at stake here, especially for Sonya. If she loses this case, she'll have to spend the next few months building a huge statue of J. C. Cramwood. In fact, *Action News* has obtained a complete copy of the specifications for the statue Cramwood wants if he wins. I quote, 'If found guilty, Sonya Sondheim will make a life-size statue of J. C. Cramwood that is two hundred feet high. It will have a helicopter pad on top of the head, a giant movie screen across the chest, and restrooms in each shoulder.'

"That's a tall order, and Sonya doesn't want to have anything to do with it. But maybe she won't have to. The scientific

DOUG IS ACTING AS IF HE HAS SOMETHING UP HIS SLEEVE, AND HE'S ABOUT TO CALL HIS LAST WITNESS. LET'S RETURN TO SCIENCE COURT FOR ALL THE ACTION.
PreSS

evidence presented so far clearly points to heat expansion as the culprit, rather than shoddy workmanship on Sonya's part."

Doug rose dramatically from behind his table. "I call Sonya Sondheim to the stand," he announced. Sonya glanced nervously at Alison and Tim, who winked reassuringly. The truth was, however, that they had seen Doug Savage at work before and knew he was always ready to pull a fast one, especially when he had been backed into a corner. They expected a desperate move from Savage, and that's just what they got.

Doug began his questioning in a sarcastic tone. "So, Sonya, you've made some pretty nice stuff over the years, haven't you?"

"Well, I like to think so," she replied.

"You've won awards, and had exhibits, and sold some of your works of art for lots of money, haven't you?" he taunted. "In fact, you're probably considered to be a pretty good all-around sculptor, right?"

"Yes," was her simple reply.

"So please tell this jury why you suddenly made something that completely fell apart. Or should I say something that fell … on people!" demanded Doug.

Sonya chose her words carefully. "It didn't fall because of anything I did. It expanded because of the heat from those powerful spotlights."

"Ha," Doug laughed mockingly. "So now you're blaming science for the disaster that befell my innocent client."

"Well, yes. And Cramwood himself for using those hot spotlights," said Sonya calmly.

"What about jealousy, Ms. Sondheim? Didn't plain old jealousy play a part in all of this?" Doug was on a roll. In fact, he took off his jacket, rolled up his sleeves, and looked directly into the jurors' eyes. "Jealousy and revenge," he continued. "The oldest story in the book." Doug swung back around and faced Sonya. "Isn't it true that the plaque didn't fall because of all this scientific mumbo jumbo? And isn't it also true that you're in love with Cramwood and want to get back at him because he spurned your advances?"

With those words the jury exploded. Judge Stone banged her gavel so hard it broke.

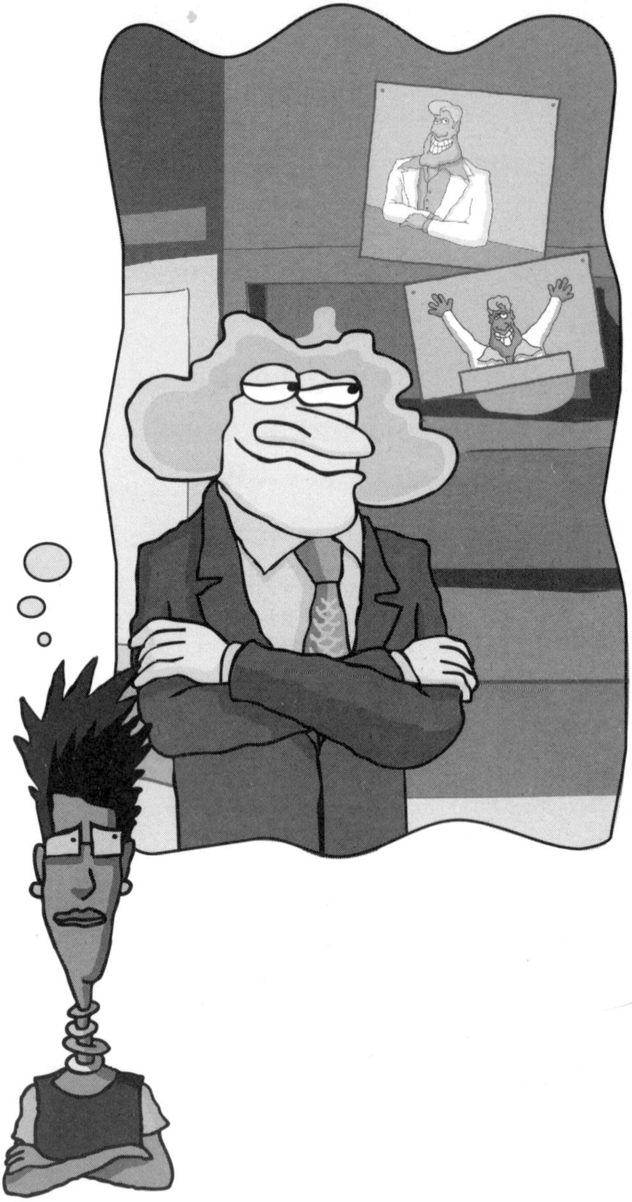

"Order, order!" she shouted. "People, calm down. Mr. Savage, just what are you up to?"

Sonya was stunned. She was more afraid than ever that she'd have to make that statue, all because of Doug Savage. Tim and Alison looked worried, too. Judge Stone continued, "Mr. Savage, you have just made a pretty strong accusation. I hope you can back it up."

"Ms. Sondheim." Doug addressed the terrified witness. "Do you remember when I went to your studio yesterday? Please tell the court what happened."

Sonya took a deep breath and composed herself. "Well, you handed me a description of the monstrosity you call a statue. You know, the one with the helicopter pad, the movie screen, and the restrooms. But when you saw a couple of pictures of Cramwood on my wall, you went skipping out the door, singing, 'I'm going to win, I'm going to win.' I thought it was awfully weird."

"Yes, Ms. Sondheim. You have pictures of Cramwood plastered all over your walls because you're in love with him. I'm right, right? And I figure that Cramwood didn't respond to your advances. I'm still right, right? So you made the frame for his plaque too small so that it would fall on his head in front of hundreds of fans eating cheese and crackers. Right, right?"

"No! That's not right!" insisted Sonya, who was now fighting mad. "I had pictures of Mr. Big Deal J. C. Cramwood on my wall because I was carving his face into a brass plaque, not because I love him. I just needed to know exactly what the guy looked like."

Doug was stunned at Sonya's testimony and didn't know what to do next. He quietly sneaked back to his seat.

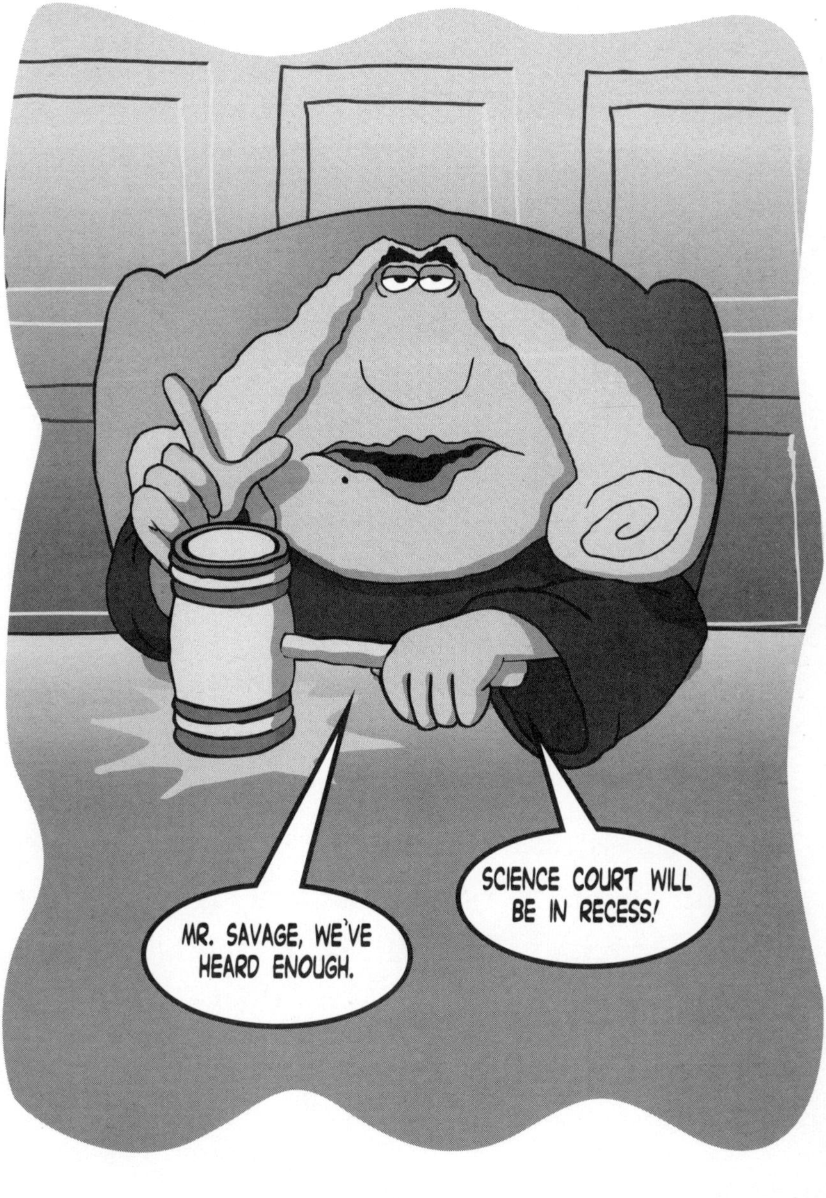
MR. SAVAGE, WE'VE HEARD ENOUGH.
SCIENCE COURT WILL BE IN RECESS!

CLOSING ARGUMENTS

Judge Stone quickly called Science Court to order and asked for closing arguments from the two attorneys. Doug began by rolling down his sleeves, adjusting his tie, putting on his jacket, and putting a smile back on his face. "Ladies and gentlemen of the jury," he said with a syrupy voice, "I can still win this case if either one of two things is true. First, if everything that Dr. Julie Bean, Dr. Henry Fullerghast, and Professor Parsons told you is wrong, then I win. Second, if Sonya Sondheim really is in love with J. C. Cramwood and really did sabotage the plaque while she was in a jealous rage, then I win again. So that's two for me and none for the other side. Vote with me, guys. You won't regret it."

Professor Parsons stood up and said, "Yeah, but I wasn't wrong, and neither were Julie Bean and Henry Fullerghast. And, oh yeah, Sonya Sondheim didn't care anything about revenge, either."

Judge Stone interrupted, saying, "Are you finished, Mr. Savage?"

"Well, I could go on . . ."

"You're finished, Doug. Now, Ms. Krempel, please enlighten us."

Alison stood beside the jury box. "Thank you, Judge Stone. Ladies and gentlemen of the jury, my client is an artist of the highest caliber, and, as we have learned today, she is unjustly accused of causing the embarrassing situation J. C. Cramwood found himself in when the plaque she made fell on him.

"Just what have we learned today? Well, heat can be transferred from hot spotlights to the things they are aimed at. We have also learned that everything expands as it is heated because the tiny particles called atoms and molecules spin faster and take up more space. And we have learned that not everything expands at the same rate. Wood, for example, expands to a lesser degree than brass when an equal amount of heat is applied.

"Finally, and most important, we have learned that it was not my client, Sonya Sondheim, who applied all that heat to the framed plaque, which caused all those atoms and molecules to spin out of control. It was not Sonya Sondheim who brought about the plunging-plaque disaster, but J. C. Cramwood himself who ordered those spotlights turned on and started the whole sequence of events.

"In fact, I've written a little poem to help you remember what I've just said. Here goes:

*Solid things seem solid,
   but look closer and they're not.*

*The particles inside are moving,
   especially when it's hot.*

*And as those babies start to spin
   around with lots of vigor,*

*They push themselves apart a bit,
   which makes the stuff grow bigger.*

*It's our understanding that
   heat will cause expanding—*

*Some things grow more,
   some things grow less,*

That's just the way it grows.

"Thank you, Ms. Krempel," said Judge Stone, relieved that the trial was nearing a conclusion. "Jurors, the case is all yours. Deliberate and get back to us."

Everyone was glad that the case had finally gone to the jury. Everyone, that is, except Stenographer Fred. Fred hadn't been able to do any sketching because of all the stenographing he'd had to do, and he was brooding. *If an attorney can be a poet, then a stenographer can be an artist*, he thought as the jury filed out.

THE VERDICT

Fred was back on the courthouse steps with his easel when Jen came by and told him that a verdict had been reached.

"What was it?" inquired Fred excitedly.

"They didn't say yet. Everyone is waiting for you," Jen told him as she motioned for him to follow her inside.

When he was in his place, Fred announced that the jury had reached a verdict and that everyone was to remain seated after it was announced.

"Why, Fred?" asked Judge Stone.

"You'll see," was his reply.

"Okay, let's hear it," ordered the judge.

The foreperson rose and read nervously from a piece of paper. "We, the jury, find the defendant not guilty of making a bad plaque and causing the movie star J. C. Cramwood embarrassment, not to mention a headache. You see, it was the heat from all of those spotlights that caused the brass plaque to expand and pop out of its frame."

"Thank you, jury, well done. Science Court is adjourned," said the judge as she banged her new gavel.

"Okay, everybody stay where you are," said Fred as he set up his easel. "Jen has promised to use my sketch of all of you on the six o'clock *Action News*, and I've only got a few hours before the deadline."

"I have more important things to do," said J. C. Cramwood as he sneaked out the back door.

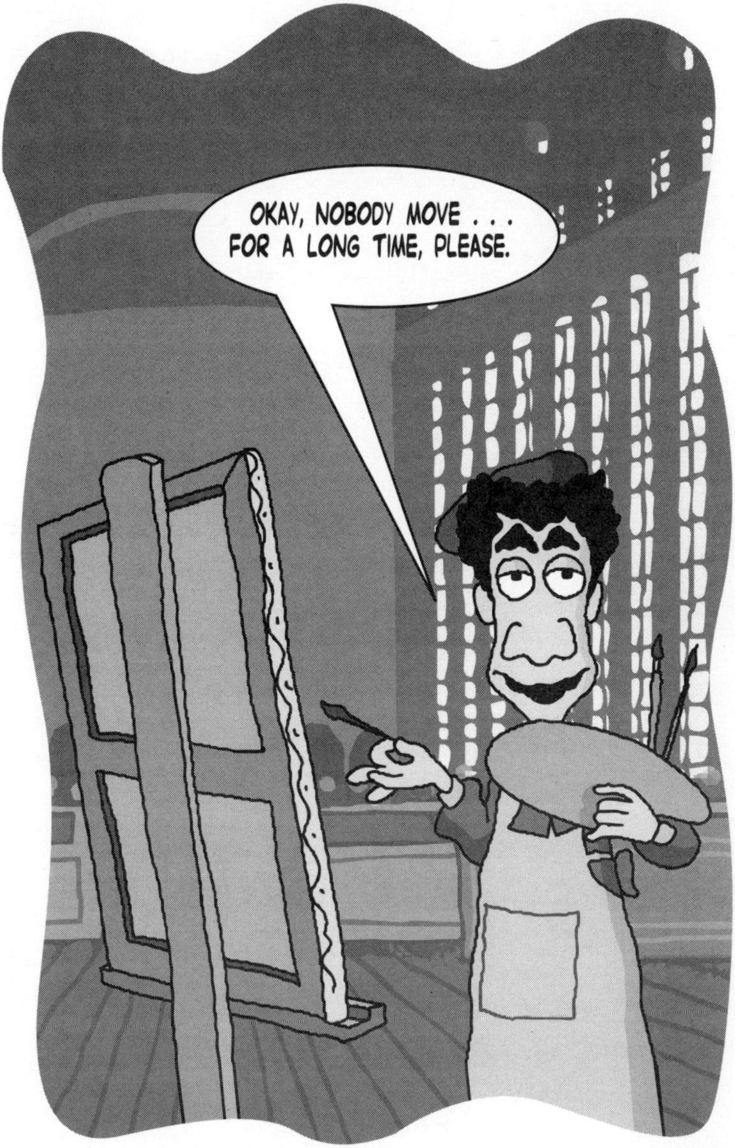
OKAY, NOBODY MOVE . . .
FOR A LONG TIME, PLEASE.

ACTIVITY
Air Expansion

DID YOU KNOW THAT AIR EXPANDS WHEN HEATED? TRY THIS EXPERIMENT.

WHAT YOU NEED:

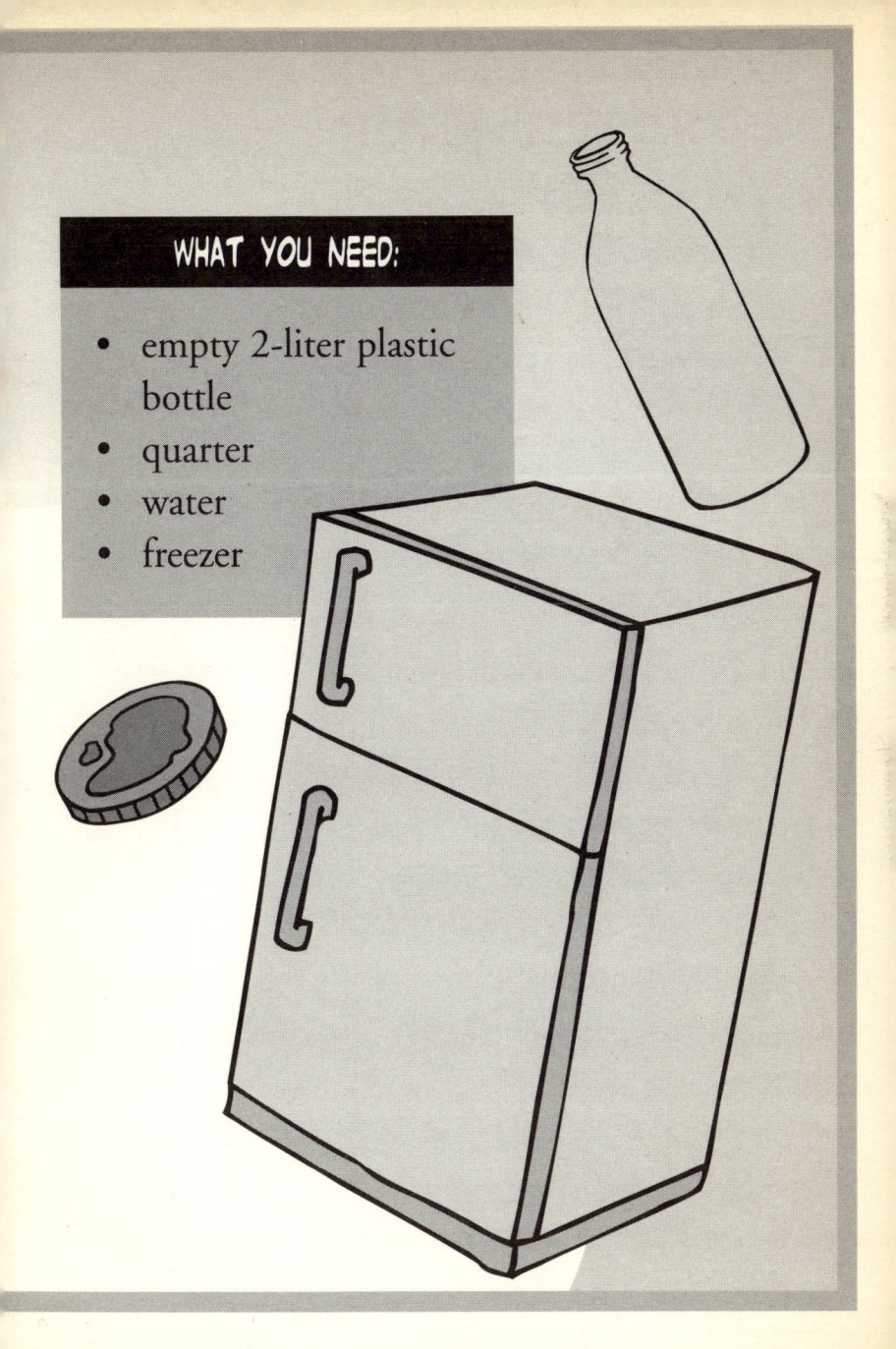

- empty 2-liter plastic bottle
- quarter
- water
- freezer

WHAT YOU DO:

1. Place the empty bottle in the freezer for at least fifteen minutes.

2. Remove the cold bottle from the freezer and stand it on a flat surface. Dip your finger in water and spread a layer of water around the rim of the bottle opening.

WHAT HAPPENS:

When the air inside the bottle heats up, it expands, forcing air out of the bottle. As the air escapes, the quarter moves and you hear a clicking sound.

3

Dip the quarter in water and immediately place it on top of the bottle. Be sure the quarter completely covers the opening of the bottle.

4

Observe the quarter and listen for any sounds.

WHAT IT PROVES:

As the cold air inside the bottle begins to warm, the molecules speed up, and the air inside the bottle starts to expand. As the air expands it creates enough pressure to raise the quarter on top of the bottle and allow air to escape. When enough air escapes, the quarter falls back and covers the opening of the bottle.

For more Science Court fun, and to find out how to bring Science Court into your classroom, visit our web site.
www.TeachTSP.com/classroom/SciCourt